Successful
Human Resource
Management
in a week

Successful
Human Resource
Management
in a week

*Graham Willcocks
and Steve Morris*

eadway · Hodder&Stoughton

British Library Cataloguing in Publication Data

A catalogue for this title is available from
the British Library

ISBN 0 340 654872

First published 1996
Impression number 10 9 8 7 6 5 4 3 2 1
Year   1999   1998   1997   1996

Typeset by Multiplex Techniques Ltd, St Mary Cray, Kent.
Printed in Great Britain for Hodder & Stoughton Educational,
a division of Hodder Headline Plc, 338 Euston Road, London
NW1 3BH by Redwood Books, Trowbridge, Wiltshire.

the Institute
of Management

F O U N D A T I O N

The Institute of Management (IM) is at the forefront of
management development and best management
practice. The Institute embraces all levels of
management from students to chief executives. It
provides a unique portfolio of services for all
managers, enabling them to develop skills and achieve
management excellence.

For information on the benefits of membership, please
contact:

Department HS
Institute of Management
Cottingham Road
Corby
Northants NN17 1TT

Tel: 01536 204222
Fax: 01536 201651

This series is commissioned by the Institute of
Management Foundation.

C O N T E N T S

∎ I N T R O D U C T I O N ∎

Fundamentally, human resource management is about people. People who work for an organisation, however, sometimes get lumped together as 'personnel'. This sometimes means that ordinary managers and supervisors automatically view anything to do with human resources as a job for the personnel professionals – as someone else's job.

Admittedly, there are times when special expertise and knowledge are needed. But increasingly, line managers have access to such expertise not as a separate function but as a form of internal consultancy. Where this happens, the day-to-day work is done by the manager or supervisor closest to the front line, backed up by advice and support from the personnel specialists.

This makes human resource management a partnership and means that every manager must be able to plan, develop and maintain their own HRM approach. Then they can play their part properly and work in harmony with the specialists.

Perhaps the most compelling point is simply that every manager and supervisor works with people. It is a rare breed of manager who has no human resources at their disposal. Managing them, like managing any resources, just isn't a task that can be left to someone else.

As you go through the week you will explore the key issues that you need to know about to play your part effectively.

Your week is set out like this:

Sunday	The helicopter view
Monday	Foundations of human resource planning
Tuesday	Looking to the future
Wednesday	Training and development
Thursday	The human side of systems
Friday	Working with the law
Saturday	Drawing the threads together

The helicopter view

Today you are going to take a helicopter view of the key aspects of human resource management (HRM) that make up the whole picture. It will help you as you work through different areas of HRM over the rest of the week.

Why HRM is at the heart of your success

An important point to consider right at the start is that HRM, by definition, is about people. It is also a positive and constructive area of management that aims to:

- prevent problems arising for and from individuals, and from having the wrong level of human resources available
- stop any problems that do emerge from growing into major dramas.

You can't have it both ways

Maybe there are some aspects of HRM that you don't have
to worry about. Perhaps some parts of it can be left entirely
to other specialist managers, possibly in the personnel
department.

To test this out, have a look at this list of responsibilities and
cross out any that have nothing to do with you.

Six key areas of HRM
1   Planning staffing levels and deployment
2   Recruitment and selection
3   Training and development
4   Appraisal
5   Health and safety
6   Procedures, especially discipline and grievance

Sorry, but this was a bit of a trick question. Any crossings-
out mean you either have nobody working for you or you
need to think again. If you have people whose performance
makes any contribution to your results, directly or
indirectly, you have a stake in all these issues. But getting
involved in these issues takes time and can sometimes be a
bit of a challenge.

Because of this, managers sometimes only want to do the
HRM parts of their job when it's easy and enjoyable. When
the going gets tough they run to the personnel department.
The message is, you can't have it both ways. When it comes
to uncomfortable situations like disciplining someone who
fails to meet the required standards, you can't abdicate
responsibility and expect someone else to pick up the pieces.
It's all part of your role.

You may not always have to do it all, though. The point is that HRM in a structured organisation is a partnership. On the one hand, there is the professional manager who deals directly and daily with the people and on the other hand, there are the other professional specialists, waiting in the wings to provide help and support.

Someone running a small business on their own probably doesn't have the luxury of a specialist department. They may have to take on the support role themselves and develop their supervisors to take on the day-to-day role.

HRM partnerships

Good management is rarely about leaping into action before engaging the brain. In all HRM situations there are steps that have to be taken if the result is going to be the right one. The steps differ depending on which aspect of HRM you're looking at, but the important point is that there is always some planning and preparation needed.

For instance, think about a specific situation. You're a front line manager and one of your team resigns. Before rushing out to advertise the job, you take the following steps.

Steps in the appointment process

1 Confirm the job is still needed because:
   - situations change and maybe the need for the job has declined since the last post-holder was appointed. They could have completed a specific project, or what they used to do by hand can now be done by a machine
   - resources are always likely to be limited, so perhaps another vacancy should take priority.

2 If the job is needed, review and confirm what results it delivers and turn them into a job specification.

3 Consider the selection criteria carefully and realistically, identifying what skills, attributes and qualifications the ideal post holder:
   - must have, or they can't do the job
   - should have, ideally
   - could have, as extras.

4 Advertise the vacancy, internally and externally, inviting applications and sending out the details.

5 Review the applications and agree the interview short list.

6 Interview the candidates.

7 Select the right one – not just the best one because that could be the best of a bad bunch; the successful candidate has to meet at least all the 'must' criteria you drew up.

Some of these steps you take yourself. For instance, you are best placed to look at whether the job is needed and is the highest priority. You may not have the final say but a reasoned and justifiable proposition from you will carry some weight with the final decision-makers.

Other steps may be taken alone by someone else who may be responsible for the wording or booking of newspaper advertisements, for instance, if you work in a large organisation.

Some steps you take together. Short-listing and interviewing generally involve more than one person, each contributing their own experience and expertise. Think it through from your own experience and write down somewhere:

- which of the steps in recruitment you take alone, in your everyday role
- which steps other people take alone, and who they are
- which steps you take jointly.

All three options are aspects of a partnership. You don't have to do everything jointly to be working together, for each other. You can apply exactly the same principles to every one of the HRM issues in the list of six key areas you saw before.

Specifying your role

The five check-lists that follow each show five crucial steps in areas of HRM responsibility. The actions will be a partnership involving generic managers and supervisors as well as specialists. You've already seen the second key area (recruitment and selection) in some detail.

Staffing levels and deployment

Often still known as 'manpower planning', despite the moves to equal opportunities, the actions commonly to be taken here are:

1 Identify the results required from the manager's area of work
2 Specify the number, skill levels and location of people needed to deliver the results
3 Review and analyse the existing resources and compare them to what was specified in (2)
4 Identify the gaps
5 Devise and implement a plan to fill the gaps

Incidentally, although you might need to look in the index under 'manpower' if you want to explore the topic in other specialist books, you will see the term 'human resource planning' used in this one.

Training and development

1 Identify training and development needs
2 Consider the alternative approaches available for delivering training and development

3 Plan action to meet the identified needs, selecting
   appropriate options to suit the individual and the
   situation
4 Deliver or arrange for the delivery of training and
   development
5 Review the effectiveness of the training and
   development

Appraisal

1 Confirm what objectives the individual has been
   aiming to achieve during the past period
2 Set up the appraisal interview and give appropriate
   notice and advance briefing
3 Review evidence about the individual's performance
   before the interview
4 Hold the interview and discuss how well the
   individual has performed
5 Record any details and set objectives for the next
   period

Health and safety

1 Identify your areas of responsibility – who is
   responsible and for what
2 Review the situation for risks and any areas below
   the required standard
3 Take the appropriate corrective action
4 Discuss specialist issues with the specialists
5 Keep monitoring and reviewing the situation

Procedures, especially grievance and discipline

1 Clarify the nature and extent of the problem
2 Confirm that everyone involved knows the exact details of the relevant procedure
3 Follow the procedure exactly as it is laid down
4 Follow all the steps and only the steps laid down in the procedure
5 Follow the procedure to the letter!

As the week progresses you'll come across these issues in more depth. It's important that you spend some time reflecting on your own role. So before you move on, identify:

- all the HRM issues you are involved in
- what others do in partnership with you on these HRM issues
- what your own role is – specifically what you have to do.

Sharp and soft edges

You can see that some HRM topics appear to have sharper edges and clearer guidelines than others. The first rule is to stick to laws, procedures and guidelines. If you think there are better ways of doing something, make out a reasoned case and present it. But keep doing it the prescribed way until the procedure changes. Don't sabotage the organisation by going your own way.

Health and safety, discipline and grievance, for example, are laid down by law and/or by the organisation's rules. Where this is the case, follow the rules.

Similarly, if the boss says you have £1,000 in a budget, don't devise plans to spend £5,000. If you do, one of your partners will get very upset. This partner is a professional who hasn't been mentioned before… the finance specialist. In every situation there will be budget constraints and this brings the finance people in as partners, either directly or through the budget allocation provided for personnel, training and so on.

It's the way that you do it
Procedures are fine, but people are not machines and this makes each HRM situation potentially unique. Anyone can stick to procedures but only people who think and care about the effect they have on others can make HRM work for everyone's benefit. The soft edges are the skills you use

in working through any of the check-lists. They are the attributes that mark out managers who make a real contribution to effective HRM from those who just go through the motions.

The sort of skills and attributes that make the difference are:

- communication skills, like interviewing, listening and constructive feedback
- skill in planning
- effective team leadership
- self-control and assertiveness.

Remember that all the aspects of human resource management that you have looked at so far are designed to:

- be of positive help to you, the individuals reporting to you and to the organisation

- prevent problems developing
- solve them as easily and painlessly as possible if
they do start.

Summary

Before tomorrow, think about where you feel you could do with improving your HRM skills and make some notes. Then, as you work through the week, you can start ticking off topics as you cover them.

Today you have looked at the wider scene, at the range of HRM issues that involve all managers and the ways in which personnel specialists and line managers work in partnership.

Tomorrow you'll explore your role in one of the key HRM issues – human resource planning – in more detail.

Foundations of human resource planning

Today is when you look at the basics of human resource planning. By tonight you will have an outline of some areas and issues you need to work on in your current arrangements. Analysis always comes before action.

People and machines

All managers look after resources, identifying what they need and how to use them to best effect. In some situations, however, it seems as if maintaining and updating the machines, equipment and buildings are a priority, while the people just plod on from day to day.

Take a situation where you have six people, one photocopier and a couple of likely scenarios.

Scenario 1

In a busy office, six administration staff work hard to process claims, invoices and tenders. There is no slack in the system. They rely heavily on the photocopier and, when it breaks down, everyone panics. The engineer is called out urgently and agrees to come immediately, either fixing the machine or installing a temporary replacement.

When it happens three or four times in a month, the money is immediately found to replace the old machine and a new, more sophisticated model appears.

Scenario 2

In the same busy office, one of the team leaves to get another job. Nobody seems very keen to get recruitment moving quickly and it feels as if there is a plot to save some money by keeping the post unfilled.

The rest of the team works hard to do the impossible and stays late, taking shorter breaks and cutting a few corners. Luckily, nothing goes wrong.

Unfortunately, there still seems to be nothing happening to replace the lost team member. Everyone keeps struggling on and that is because they take their work seriously. As long as the team's goodwill lasts, nobody outside the section would know from the output that there was a problem.

You may feel this is how a lot of organisations operate… and unfortunately it is. Lose a machine and it's an instant response, but managers are not so quick to respond when it comes to losing staff. They very quickly get used to being short-staffed and muddling through until it becomes the norm. Then, when someone does complain that more people are needed, the reply comes back that you've always managed so far, so there can't be a problem.

The goodwill, however, does eventually run out, and when it finally does, all manner of problems surface. Other people leave, or stop co-operating so readily. The effective team breaks down and everyone – individuals, manager and the organisation – suffers. This second scenario is a classic example of poor use of human resources. It illustrates a lack of any real planning or monitoring.

Essentials of human resource planning

The aim is to achieve the results you need by having:

- the right number of people
- with the right skills
- in the right place
- at the right time

As a diagram it is a cycle that looks like this:

If you explore this cycle in detail, some key points emerge.

Start with the objectives
Everything a manager does has to support the organisation's objectives. If it doesn't, there is something fundamentally wrong. The results needed from a section or department are generally set out as their specific objectives, and this is the base line in human resource planning.

Planning what people you need only makes sense if you know what results you are meant to achieve, and have agreed your objectives. Making sure this first stage is covered may look obvious, but sometimes it's the obvious that gets forgotten.

Key point
Make sure you're absolutely clear on your objectives.

Who do we need?
The objectives give you a frame of reference, a sort of picture, that allows you to work back and clarify the human resources you need. To do any job you need the right resources, a particular number of people who are there when needed with the appropriate skills.

Three questions
Ask yourself:
1 What would happen if there weren't enough people?
2 What would happen if there were too many?
3 What would happen if the number was right, but they had the wrong mix of skills?

Some of the answers again might seem obvious. That is because they are. However, it doesn't stop them being potential problems, especially when the obvious gets overlooked.

Too few people
Having too few people leaves a simple physical problem, but understanding the problem in detail gives you the ammunition to counter anyone who seems to think it's a way of saving money. It might cut the wages bill, but it adds to other direct and indirect costs enormously.

Imagine you need ten people, all doing the same work, and you have nine. There are only two deceptively simple possibilities: either everything gets done, 90% well; or not everything can be done and 10% or so is going to be left. This is an extremely important and powerful point to carry with you. You cannot physically produce the required results to the appropriate standard if you don't have enough people. Any sports team that has someone sent off might hold the line for a time, but eventually they'll crack and lose.

Sometimes though, short-term measures are taken to temporarily mask the problem, such as:

- people work overtime, and that costs more per unit of output than normal time
- expensive agency staff or casual employees are drafted in, and they need training to be anything like as effective as someone who really knows the job and is committed.

Alternatively, the problem is ignored and everyone works like they did in scenario 2 for a while, until:

- stress and discontent sets in and brings even greater problems in the long run
- staff turnover goes up, adding to recruitment and training costs
- commitment and motivation go down, leading to problems that take up management time and produce nothing extra
- quality suffers and the organisation's customers and clients notice the fact… and go to competitors.

The problem gets worse if the operations are more complex.

If you control more than two processes, you might have enough people in one and too few in another. This leads to bottlenecks, as products and services clog up the system and have to wait. You have one group short of people and another short of work, because they can't pass any more down the line. You see the results when waiting for a meal to be served in a restaurant, or queuing for one hygienist supporting three dentists.

Also there is a danger that, when the problem is tackled, the wrong people are lost:

Cutting from the bottom

As the recession forced companies to shed workers in the 1980s, a food processing firm was one that was hit. The top managers assumed they must keep all the managers and specialists, so the cuts started at the bottom with clerical staff and manual employees. The trouble was that the work hadn't changed. There was still a need for typing, filing and manual handling of products.

The net result was that everyone ended up doing bits of the next job down. Instead of a relatively inexpensive clerk doing the filing, it had to be done by a senior clerk, and products had to be moved either by people leaving their machines or by charge hands and supervisors. Naturally, time spent doing routine jobs ate into the time they should have spent doing their own work, so more was lost than gained in the end.

Having enough people sounds so obvious it shouldn't need saying, but when you look at the impact a staff shortage has on staff morale, the reputation of the organisation and its long-term financial strength, you can see it is of immense importance.

Key point

Examine your operations regularly to make sure there are enough people in all parts of the process. Look out for overtime and other costly options.

Too many people

Unfortunately there are cases of managers playing it safe and having a few extra people just in case, or building empires by taking on more and more staff. It's bad management. Having too many people is clearly wasteful, because they have to be paid and they need space, administration and all the other extras that make up personnel costs.

But it doesn't stop there. Having people with time on their hands leads to problems. People feel they aren't stretched and they get bored. Motivation, morale and commitment all suffer, and you can end up with a lot of people producing less than a smaller number could deliver.

> **Key point**
>
> Make sure you don't have too many people – look
> around with a fresh eye and try and see the situation
> objectively.

The right place at the right time

This is fairly obvious. It's no use having twenty people in
Bolton if most of the work is in Bristol. Nor is it sensible to
employ more than a skeleton staff at night in a rural 24-hour
filling station.

Inside a department, one operation could need more people,
even just for a couple of hours. In a bakery, for instance,
someone away on jury service could cause a bottleneck. But
you could sort out the problem temporarily by shifting the
balance of staff between different operations, to keep them
running smoothly. The chances are that you can see this sort
of situation coming and can plan for it.

> **Key point**
>
> Look at output figures and other statistics, and talk to
> people to get a clear picture of where and when the
> pressure points are.

The right skills

You might have enough bodies, but they might not be able
to do the right things. You're going to look at this issue in
some detail on Wednesday, when you explore training and
development. But for now the simple message is that

everyone has to be competent to do their part of the task, so their combined efforts produce the required results.

Key point

Look at job descriptions and what happens day to day, and identify exactly what skills, attributes and knowledge people need.

Cover these key points and you will know who you need. Putting the details into a simple framework helps you to see the whole picture. It is useful to draw up a chart on the following lines, filling in the spaces.

Objectives	
Number of people needed	
Special time and place considerations	
Skills needed	

Who do we have now?

So far you have covered the first two stages in the cycle: the objectives and the analysis of what you need. If you look at the human resources in place now, it is easy to compare what you already have with what you need. This throws up any gaps.

There are no magic answers to analysing what you have now. It is a straightforward process of listing how many people you have, where and when they work and what skills they possess. The simplest way to approach it is to use the same chart you used for reviewing what you need, changing one or two words. The objectives stay the same, but it then becomes:

- how many people you have
- where and when they work
- what skills they bring with them.

Before moving on to tomorrow, make sure you have a clear picture of where your current resources match what you need and, most importantly, exactly what the gaps are.

Summary

Today you have looked at the analytical side of human resource planning, using a cycle that allows you to tackle each component issue simply and clearly. Going through the stages in the cycle has given you a picture of any gaps that cause you either a real or potential problem.

Tomorrow you will look at a vital added factor, which is that nothing stands still. You have analysed the situation in today's human resources, but this is likely to change and you have to analyse and prepare for changes. Once you have a vision of the future you can plan to bridge both the existing and the emerging gaps.

Looking to the future

Today is about two main issues:

- anticipating human resource needs so that you aren't caught out by concentrating only on the here and now
- putting together a human resources plan.

Still in analysis

Reviewing the current situation is fine, but getting the balance of human resources right today doesn't necessarily mean it will be right tomorrow. Change at work has never been faster, more wide-ranging or fundamental, and it constantly alters the human resource needs of all parts of the organisation. If you look at the cycle diagram we identified yesterday, you will see that the top box says, 'What are the objectives *now*'. The word *now* implies that they may have changed since you first started the cycle. Therefore the rest of the steps have to be revisited to fit any change in objectives.

The trick is to see change coming and accommodate it, rather than wait for it to strike and then panic. This might mean you have to spend valuable time thinking rather than doing, and some managers find this to be a problem.

All managers are busy. Some feel they are so busy coping with today's crises that there isn't time to forecast and plan for tomorrow's. It's the *Titanic* syndrome – 'I haven't got time to stand on deck looking for icebergs… I'll deal with them when I meet them'. And we all know what happened to the *Titanic*!

Forecasting and planning

These are two words that sometimes get mixed up, although they're quite different. Think about it in the context of the weather. Nobody can plan the weather, because that implies an element of control over whether it rains or not. But forecasting it is a huge industry.

Forecasting is a best guess, based on past experience, knowledge and extrapolation. Once you know the forecast you can plan accordingly, either drawing up initial plans or revising what you have already decided.

Making plans without looking ahead is dangerous. You could plan to go to the beach, but if you don't listen to the weather forecast that predicts rain, the day will be a disaster. If you take account of the forecast, you can change the plan, saying, 'Let's do something else today and go to the beach when it clears up'. Effective management of human resources relies on same mixture of forecasts and plans.

Steps in forecasting human resource needs

Forecasting means you:

- identify some factors for review
- gather information on those factors
- look at what has happened before
- think about any cause and effect – when x happened in the past, y almost always has resulted
- check out your assumption that it is likely to happen again
- make plans based on the results.

It isn't an exact science, but the benefits are a great deal higher than the costs. Any intelligence is better than none.

How do you apply the forecasting process to your own human resource planning system? Simply follow the steps of a PESTLE analysis. This is a comprehensive process already used in some organisations to spot changes and identify their potential impact.

Factors for review – PESTLE analysis
You won't be surprised to hear that PESTLE is a series of initials that spell out a standard set of factors for review, the first step in forecasting. They stand for:

Political
Economic
Social
Technological
Legal
Environmental

Virtually all the issues that affect human resource planning fit into one or more of these headings – even in a small business.

The chip shop

A chip shop owner had to change the staffing arrangements because each of the factors changed.
P Government policy introduced subsidies for young employees – so the shop took on more youngsters.
E A local factory closing down hit the local economy and, although it meant people had less to spend, business went up as customers turned to chips

instead of more expensive alternatives. Therefore, more staff were needed.

S Eating out became more fashionable, so part of the shop was turned into a sparkling restaurant area with staff required to give table service.

T The old frying machines were replaced by electronically controlled ones, so staff needed training in the new ways.

L Health and hygiene regulations were introduced, so all staff had to go on a course and get a certificate.

E The council clamped down on litter, so somebody was needed to take on the role of regularly making sure that the pavement outside was clean and tidy.

The difference between good business practice and bad can be measured by whether the chip shop owner waited until each issue became reality, or took action in advance. The owner could have anticipated each one because:

- the government's employment subsidies had been advertised on TV and at Job Centres
- there had been redundancies and rumours of the factory closure for several months
- the local council had published a survey report on eating out trends as part of their economic development activity
- the sales representative from the equipment supplier had provided brochures and technical specifications during the negotiations, and even explained the courses they ran for customers

- the health and hygiene regulations had been talked about in the trade press for months before they came into effect
- the local paper had reported council debates on the mess outside the local burger bar and the way the council was determined to tighten up litter controls for all take-away food shops.

Carrying out PESTLE analysis

There are some simple rules for identifying which potential changes will affect your human resource planning. Ideally it is done in a group of colleagues, so that the breadth of knowledge and discussion is as wide as possible, and ideas can spark off other ideas. Once you have briefed everyone on what you are doing, the process follows these steps:

1 Look at each factor in turn and consider all the possible issues that might affect the organisation and your part in it. For instance, under technology, you might know of:
   - a new material or some equipment that is becoming standard within the industry that you need to think about
   - refinements in computers or programs that are spreading in your industry, or are already coming to other departments and look as if they're coming to yours.
2 Discuss the details of the potential change – based on past experience and a projection of what seems to be the likely course of events.
3 Draw up a 'what if' scenario and a contingency strategy to handle the impact on human resources.

4 Start planning or, if appropriate, talk to a senior manager
   about the chances of what you are proposing, to check
   out whether there are factors like budgets or policies that
   will influence the likelihood of the change happening.

   Don't just sit there...

   ... do it. Do it for your own area of operations, looking
   at what will affect you in the next eighteen months. Put
   the information alongside the gaps you identified
   yesterday.

You now have the outline of a complete picture, one that
sets out the known gaps in your present human resources
and also identifies the potential gaps that you will have to
cope with. If the results show that the number of people is
wrong, whether it's too many or too few for now or for the
foreseeable future, you have to:

  • start thinking about what action to take, if you have
    the decision-making authority
  • put together a proposal that explains how you came
    to your conclusions and justifies action by the
    appropriate people.

It could be, though, that the overall number is about right,
and what is needed is some shift in roles, some flexibility in
the demarcation between jobs and the way people work.

Developing a flexible approach

The analytical approach to human resource planning gives
you all the basic information you need. But as you consider

potential future changes, stop and think about the changes in the way work has been structured in recent years. You'll see that a flexible approach is normal these days. Go back a few years and this wasn't the case. Rigid and clear boundaries between separate jobs would have been normal because:

- most of the work was done by direct employees, organised in specialist and separate groups
- demarcation lines were clear and reinforced by union agreements and management territories
- people stuck to their own skills and crafts, as they had many years of service and were deeply skilled in a specific set of tasks.

If you took on an extra maintenance electrician, for instance, it had no impact on how many mechanical maintenance staff were employed. The different disciplines didn't cross over to handle 'other people's work'.

Times have changed and are going to continue to do so at a faster and faster rate. Words like multi-skilling and de-skilling have become commonplace, meaning that one person often takes on a range of tasks, thus blurring the old demarcation lines. The future is going to change even further. Writers and management gurus like Charles Handy and Tom Peters are clear that, in the organisations of the future, only a very small number of core staff will be needed. Much of the work will be done by subcontractors, consultants, temporary staff and project teams.

Look around organisations and you'll see outside contractors doing jobs that were always done by direct employees.

In-house services

As compulsory competitive tendering has taken hold in
public services, many of the departments that were
providing services like street sweeping, catering,
security and cleaning have lost out to private
organisations. Others, though, have retained the work
in the open market, in the face of stiff competition.

They have done this by adding new skills to those they
already had, adopting market-based and customer-
focused approaches alongside their established
technical ability. The successful in-house organisations
have looked ahead and developed their existing
workforce as the basis for the new arrangements,
rather than scrapping everything and starting again.

Many managers want to preserve their teams and the status
quo. This is fine, and it makes sense to build on existing
foundations rather than demolish a basically sound
structure for the sake of it. But denying reality and resisting
all change in employment patterns does not make the issue
disappear.

To maintain your influence on the employment trends in
your own operations, you have to take a cold hard look at
the options. Neither you nor the people who look to you for
a lead can afford for you to opt out. As the saying goes, 'You
can't win it if you're not in it'.

All this highlights how important it is to look ahead, to do forecasting and analysis, in order to identify possible strategies that will deliver the results you need. You may have to approach the future with a clean sheet of paper. It isn't enough to think in terms of the job titles that exist now. Instead, look for occasions when it might be appropriate to:

- retrain existing employees to broaden their roles
- contract out short-term or specialist services to an external supplier
- increase flexibility through an increase in part-time or casual work.

For many managers the preferred option is to develop the existing resources, and this may mean looking at people through fresh eyes. Rather than pigeon-holing people and labelling them with job titles, see them as individuals with the potential to learn new skills and techniques. Then, as long as you look ahead and don't wait until the problem arrives, you can deal with many of the challenges that the future will throw at you.

Options for action

What you decide to do has to be related to your own situation, and it's hard to give general pointers. However, imagine a situation where you have:

- eight skilled operators on old machines
- only one operator who can run a computerised machine
- new computerised machines planned for next year.

You have only three options:

- sack the existing people and take on eight new ones
- work out a training strategy to upgrade their skills
- close your eyes and pretend it isn't happening.

Don't choose option 3!

Option 1 potentially wastes all the other knowledge those people have about the organisation and the way it works. This option is also guaranteed to remove goodwill from other staff and turn the organisation into one where management is seen as uncaring, expedient and untrustworthy. That doesn't leave many options… so obviously option 2 comes out as favourite.

However, there are situations where retraining is not possible, such as where the change is more radical and involves a new direction entirely. For instance, a move from running your own transport fleet to contracting out the entire function almost certainly means redundancies. The actual decisions have to be taken in the light of the circumstances prevailing at the time.

The staffing plan

It's time to put together everything you have uncovered so far into one outline plan for the next eighteen months. Remember, the plan may need to change if the external circumstances change, but at least with a plan you have a starting point, something to evaluate and decide whether it still fits the bill.

Draw up your plan using the following headings:

1 Our current objectives and any likely changes
2 Number of people required to deliver the objectives, broken down as appropriate into job roles, functions and tasks
3 The skills needed by those people in those roles
4 The gaps between what there is and what we need
5 Potential for retraining and upgrading skills
6 Suggested action to bridge all the gaps

It's more than half an hour's work to do a plan like this. It takes time, research and a lot of thought, but the plan you end up with will help enormously in by keeping your operations flowing smoothly and avoiding problems, bottlenecks and skill shortages.

Summary

Today you have extended the basic human resource planning you started yesterday, adding some techniques for handling the uncertainty of the future. The staffing plan you have should make life a lot easier in times to come, especially when you update it on a rolling basis every six months.

Tomorrow you're going to move on and look at a crucial HRM issue that helps bridge the gaps between what there is and what is needed. This is training and development.

Training and development

Human resource planning gives you the big picture – the long-term framework of intelligence and information you need to keep everything moving. It provides the context for today's topic – the development of a system for training and developing people so they can perform at the required standards.

Huge amounts of time and money are wasted every year on training. This doesn't imply that training should be scrapped. Training itself certainly is not a waste; the waste comes when the wrong people are trained in the wrong things, often at the expense of the right things for the right people. Getting it right is hard and requires analysis and planning.

The cycle at work in training and development looks similar to the one you saw earlier.

This cycle carries all the main components of an initiative you may have heard of. *Investors in People* is a standard for simple good HRM practice. There is essentially nothing new about it, except the standard against which organisations are assessed.

This standard measures how well human resource development (HRD) is operated by an organisation. The organisation has to demonstrate that it has workable and effective systems which ensure that:

- everyone knows what the organisation aims to do, and what individual people have to be able to do as their contribution to overall success
- training and development needs are identified, so that what is provided is planned and prioritised
- the training and development is provided once planned
- the organisation and the individuals assess whether it worked.

Investors in People specifies that managers should be competent in identifying training needs and delivering some training, thus sharing responsibility for the training and development of their people. Obviously, running specialised courses might need a qualified trainer, but working out the needs and doing some of the front line training is best done by the person nearest the real situation... and that's you.

Training and development needs

You have seen gaps mentioned a lot so far. Here come some more, because training and development needs are gaps, or:

...problems, deficiencies or shortcomings that can be removed through training and development.

There are two sides to this. One is the existence of a problem or a gap, and the other is that it can be sorted out through training and development. If the problem is, say, a health and safety issue that can only be removed by a new fire escape, all the training in the world can't help. And the needs aren't just about individuals who seem to require a shot in the arm. Identifying training and development needs means looking systematically at deficiencies on three separate, but related levels. They are:

- the organisation
- the occupation
- the individual.

Organisational level
Organisations have a responsibility for setting and meeting objectives. Organisational training and development needs are any problems, gaps or deficiencies that threaten to

scupper the achievement of the objectives, and can be removed through training or development.

The following is an example of how one firm set some organisational objectives and why.

Le grand training need

A firm of lawyers decided to move into the international property conveyancing market but only the chairman spoke French – and everyone needed to if the firm was to succeed. The key people attended classes and learnt the language, followed later by other staff. It was an organisation-wide deficiency that training was able to overcome.

Occupational level

This covers everyone doing the same specific occupation or job. The machine operators are a case in point, as was the introduction of the health and hygiene certificate in the chip shop example. The hygiene regulations that came in state that everyone handling or involved with food has to have passed an examination and gained a certificate.

Individual level

Anyone who is fully competent and knows exactly how the organisation works may not have any training and development needs. But even someone coming to a new job with the right qualifications, say an HGV licence, has gaps in their knowledge of how this firm operates and what its systems are.

Other gaps occur in issues like:

* team working
* communication skills
* customer care.

Customer care

The manager of a high street bank noticed a sharp rise in the number of complaints about how customers were treated when they rang in with a query. The number of customers leaving the bank for a competitor was up, and new accounts were down. People were talking about their experiences around town, and the branch's reputation was suffering.

The problem was across the board. It centred on staff not seeming to know the bank's own systems and being rude and abrupt. However, one member of staff was mentioned more than the others. The manager sat down, looked at the training and development needs at all three levels and wrote this:

The problems for the organisation – the branch – are:
* *lost business from existing accounts*
* *lost business from potential new customers*
* *a bad name in the town.*

The occupational needs are:
- *knowledge of systems*
- *low levels of customer care.*

On an individual level:
- *the member of staff with the most complaints communicates badly and projects the wrong image.*

You can see the pattern, linking all three levels. But what really shows up is that the organisational needs, expressed as problems, come first. Had the manager started with what looked like the obvious issue, the individual, nothing would have really changed. Needs at the other levels would have been missed and would have remained as problems.

Don't just sit there…

…think hard about what changes are going to have an impact on your future operations and make detailed notes on your organisational and occupational training and development needs. Link it into the staffing plan you put together yesterday.

What you have looked at in organisational and occupational needs sits right at the centre of this good practice. You can see how closely the first two points match the work you have done so far. But there is a link still missing. It's the individual.

The individual focus

Looking at organisational and occupational needs is fine, but the individual needs to be part of the process. You can determine the overall needs, but each person must have the chance to discuss with you what their own training and development needs are.

Shotguns and rifles

In a printing works the department manager worked out the training and development needs of the staff, taking the organisational view only and deciding that everybody ought to have a course on basic business costings.

The supervisor, though, talked to everyone first, and found that one person was doing an Open University Business Finance module and another had completed initial accountancy exams before entering printing. A third had run their own business and knew a great deal about costing.

Both were right in their own way; there was an overall need for training on costing although for some individuals it certainly wasn't a priority. Sending those individuals on a course that assumed they knew nothing would have been:

- a waste of money that could have gone on more relevant training
- a waste of time – theirs and the organisation's
- frustrating and counter-productive.

The shotgun approach – firing at everyone with one cartridge – hits some people and misses others. The problem is that it might not hit the ones it should, whereas the ones it hits might not need it. The rifle approach – taking aim before firing the shot – makes sure that the right target gets hit.

The appraisal process
Performance appraisal is perhaps the most powerful way of checking on individuals' training and development needs. This is another cycle that has the following components.

Identify training and
development
needs and plan
action jointly

Give constructive
feedback

At the end of the
interview, negotiate
and agree specific
targets with the
individual

Discuss how well
they have done
against the targets

Maintain a watching
brief and deliver the
training and
development
agreed

Prepare yourself
and the individual

Set up the
next appraisal
interview

The process works like this.

Set up the interview   Prepare yourself by looking at the targets you agreed with the individual last time. Remind the person you're appraising of the process, the sort of meeting it is and when and where it is to be. You need to:

• collect information on their activity
• think about your own observations
• check any statistics or reports that might help.

They need to do the same, so when you meet you are talking about the same issues.

Discuss results   Each person has the chance to explain how well things have gone in their judgement. The aim is to identify strengths and weaknesses, so as to recognise the strengths and help remove the weaknesses. Constructive feedback is telling someone what your view of their performance is, so that it helps them make improvements rather than hurting them and putting them on the defensive.

It is a difficult set of skills, but it can be developed. You'll see more about this tomorrow.

Plan training and development action   Having identified the strengths and weaknesses, draw up an agreed plan, with objectives, for overcoming the weaknesses.

Set targets for next time   Devise some achievable but challenging targets they can go for by the next interview. Derive them from the key result areas in their job description – the really important aspects of their work.

The real purpose of appraisal isn't for you to have a go at them; it's to find ways for them to improve their skills and their performance. Interviews normally take place at intervals of between six and twelve months, so if something is going wrong between interviews you should spot it in your normal watching brief as part of your everyday management role. When you do, sort it out there and then – don't leave it to fester or get forgotten.

Also between interviews, the training and development action you agreed with them takes place. The benefit of planning training through appraisal is that what you agree and plan is certain to come out of real work situations and be appropriate for the individual and the organisation.

For a closer look at appraisals, you might like to read *Successful Appraisals in a Week* by Di Kamp.

Delivering the training and development plan

There are some criteria for worthwhile training and development. Any such activity is worthwhile – and only worthwhile – if it:

- solves a problem
- increases the level of knowledge of the employee
- raises the individual's technical competence
- adds to their range of personal skills and the extent of their self-awareness
- makes complex issues simpler and easier to understand
- allows for continuous improvement.

In other words, it has to improve their performance, for their own benefit and for that of the organisation. This means learning something new – and that introduces another cycle.

The learning cycle
This cycle is widely referred to in the world of training and development. But it isn't especially clever. It's the sort of approach children use without even knowing it, when they learn to roller skate.

Put simply, what the cycle says is that every practical experience is an opportunity for learning, as long as the individual

- thinks about what happened (what went well, what didn't)
- works out why it happened like it did
- thinks about what could improve it next time, avoiding the same mistakes and trying some new tactics
- tries it out again… and goes round the cycle again.

This cycle helps individuals to devise strategies to repeat what went well and change what didn't. You can try it for yourself.

Learning from experience

1 Think of something you did today – anything at work. It might be a meeting, a report, or even how you handled someone who stopped you getting on with your work.

2 Sort out what happened by listing some of the results of the activity. Maybe it took too long, or you couldn't get rid of someone, or the meeting achieved its purpose. Think of some successful outcomes and some that need improving.

3 Now work out why they happened; why you got the results you did. Did you act in a certain way, or were you unable to handle a particular individual? If so, why?

4 Now work out some sort of strategy for improving
what needs improvement, having given yourself a
pat on the back for the good results. (This is where
training and development activity fits in – if you
aren't sure how to do better, you need to learn
something new.)
5 Finally, try it out. It won't be perfect, but it will be
better, and next time you'll iron out even more of the
wrinkles.
Now go back to the beginning.

The range of development options you could choose from at
stage 4, when helping someone decide how to improve their
performance, includes:

- courses, workshops and seminars
- reading books and articles
- job rotation

- shadowing someone else
- coaching, one-to-one
- using open and distance learning materials
- watching television or videos, or listening to radio or audio tapes
- interactive video, or computer-based learning.

These and other means are all helpful as development tools. They can all meet the list of criteria for worthwhile training and development. What matters is that the activity works, in terms of the results for the individual and the organisation.

Summary

Today you have fitted training and development into the human resource plan. By identifying the needs and planning appropriate action, you have filled in virtually all the gaps in the initial analysis.

Tomorrow you look at some of the personal skills you need to make these systems and processes work effectively.

The human side of systems

So the systems are in place, but HRM is about far more than just systems. Today the spotlight turns on you and on the way you communicate with and handle people within your HRM role. Put simply, all the systems in the world are only as good as the people making them work.

HRM in fact involves a lot of interpersonal skills. Just think about it. For a start HRM involves discussing and agreeing plans, giving feedback and fighting your corner. A bad communicator is unlikely to be successful at HRM.

The main areas to look at are:

- clarifying key result areas
- helping people through the use of standards and objectives (targets)
- giving constructive feedback.

These skills all form part of effective appraisal, and are essential in maintaining effective day-to-day relations.

Key result areas

Ask yourself this question:

How do you and your people know what they are expected to achieve?

It's an important question and one that any manager with an HRM brief needs to answer.

If you can be clear about the key result areas of a person's work then you can start measuring their success and giving them sensible and useful feedback. You can also use your key result areas to target both people and other resources. Key result areas are also likely to be a major topic of discussion at appraisals. In short, they stop you being too general and will give you a focus.

With key result areas you can reach agreement on what you are aiming for – the results – and with this you go about managing your human resources.

And your job is to make absolutely sure that:

- everyone knows what their key result areas are
- everyone agrees and shares an understanding of them
- everyone works towards them
- you have planned your human resources to make sure you get the results.

What are key result areas?
Key result areas are in fact pretty self explanatory.

1 Key result areas are the most important bits of the job description. They are why that particular job was invented in the first place. They can also change as the nature of the work changes over time.
2 Key result areas help everyone focus on priorities; they help to get the important results first and to use time and resources effectively.
3 They have to come from organisational goals – the key results of individuals also need to plug into the key results for the organisation. If they don't, they're off-beam.

4 They fit neatly into appraisal, because they help you to define really worthwhile performance objectives for the coming period.

5 They fit neatly into human resource planning. If you are clear about your key result areas then you can plan to deliver them by getting the right people in the right place at the right time.

What are the key results for your team?

Setting standards and targets

So, looking at some key result areas is one way of helping to focus on what your people should be doing and of spotting if you are going off-course.

Another way to help focus your team is to set standards and targets that everyone understands and works to.

This is actually a key part of HRM. If you can set sensible standards and targets with your people, then you can:

- measure how well they perform
- give them feedback
- use these standards and targets as a kind of team map to measure progress
- use them as a major motivating tool – people will strive to meet a standard and to exceed it.

The following check-list will help you think through some of the issues.

Understanding standards and targets

1 Standards are standard – they set out the minimum acceptable level of performance in any given job. For instance, all typists have to do two reports a day, at 80 wpm, with no errors.

2 Individuals are not standard – some are below
   (especially new ones) and some are really or
   potentially above the standard.
3 Don't expect new people to be at the standard by
   magic, and don't hold the others back and limit them
   to the minimum standard. Treat them as individuals.
4 Don't set the same targets for everyone at their
   appraisal.

Look at the following diagram. It shows a standard and two
team members in relation to it. The diagram represents the
performance of two people – person **A** and person **B**.

What relevance do you think it would have for you as a
human resource manager? What do you think has happened
in the diagram?

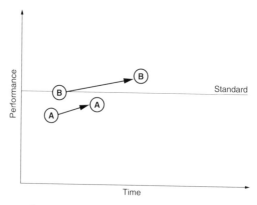

The diagram shows just how important it is to treat people
as individuals and how you can use standards to improve
your team's performance. As you can see the standard
remains the same, but the actual performance of the people
differs.

A is a new employee and is below standard. They don't know all the ropes yet, so this time you would need to agree with them a realistic target (objective) to get them nearer the standard. Next time, you could raise the target again so the improvement is continuous and incremental.

B is an old hand, coasting at the standard. They're going to get bored and lose morale if they aren't stretched, so get them motivated and give them a higher target. Then they will get more satisfaction, and the organisation (you) will get better results.

What standards have you set for your people?
How do you measure people against the standards?
How do you use standards to improve performance?

Constructive feedback

Finally, and probably most importantly, HRM is about giving good feedback.

Sure, standards and targets are important and key result areas are a useful way of giving you a focus. But at the heart of HRM is feedback, and this means telling your people:

- how well they are doing
- helping them to improve
- continuously developing them.

As a human resource manager you use feedback in a variety of arenas including appraisals.

Constructive feedback is one of the lost skills of management. It is the only way to let people see where they can improve. They know for themselves where they make obvious mistakes, but the outsider's view gives information that can help them do better.

So, what constitutes constructive feedback?

Characteristics of constructive feedback

- Constructive feedback is a set of characteristics and skills that can be learnt, developed and applied. It is not something you are born with.
- Remember, constructive does not mean the same as positive.
- You can and must give negative feedback about someone's performance that needs improving. The secret is to give it constructively.

Constructive feedback means:

- giving people information and facts about their performance that will help them analyse what happened and plan to do better, if appropriate

- giving them both the good side and the bad side in relevant proportions

- giving them the facts in a way that does not block them from listening and accepting the message

In other words, they want honest feedback from someone concerned enough about them to tell them the truth. It is important to work on what you say and how you say it.

Try this for size

Look at these two short examples. Make notes about which one you feel will have the greater impact on Jane's performance and why.

1

Jane. I've called you in because of the embarrassing meeting you ran yesterday. Now, I must speak my mind. It was appalling.

There's no chance people will want to come to another meeting. Believe me it's going to cost me more than a few drinks. The room was terrible too, with those hard chairs and the draft. Having a cold didn't help – I could hardly hear you!

Next time I'll choose someone else. I hope you take this in the spirit intended. What do you think?

2

Jane... thanks for your time – I just want to give you some feedback on the meeting and give you a chance to tell me your thoughts too.

Your preparation was good although I got a bit lost in the middle. Possibly in future it could be worth simplifying the information a little. I would have found some visual aids helpful too, and that would have helped you rest your voice.

I know how hard it is to get everyone together – so full marks for that – but I thought the room was a little uncomfortable. Anyway, think about it and let me know if I can help.

What do you think?

Both people giving feedback were at the same meeting. But the way they gave feedback was fundamentally different. Almost certainly you feel that the second approach is likely to have more impact.

Essentially, feedback is a destructive experience when it:

- gets the receiver's back up
- makes them defend their position
- fails to give them something positive to work on.

In **1** the feedback was pathetic and insulting. You may well have been on the receiving end of this kind of feedback. It won't do much to help improve things next time.

In **2** there are the characteristics of constructive feedback. These are:

- Try and start with something positive – there was bound to be something good. It means that they will listen far more readily to the negative points if you have opened up with a positive comment.
- Own the feedback – say 'I felt, I saw, I think' and not 'everyone feels' or 'they must have thought…' After all, you don't know what everyone else thinks. Using an 'I' statement increases the power of the feedback, makes you think carefully what to say and makes it easier to be factual.
- Avoid criticising things that can't be changed – 'it's a pity you had a cold.'
- Make observations not assumptions. Say, 'I noticed that you were shaking a little…' and not, 'You were obviously the nervous type.'

- Be descriptive rather than judgemental: 'The overhead projector slides were a little small for me to read' and not 'The slides weren't very good'. They need to know what exactly happened if they are to improve, and saying it wasn't very good doesn't tell them anything except your opinion.
- Respect their right to ignore the feedback.
- End your feedback on a positive.
- Always give them the opportunity to make comments and suggestions about how they feel it went.

Timing the feedback

As well as these factors, there are some issues of timing. It is never the right time to give someone feedback if they don't want it. They won't accept it and all you will do is make things worse.

Don't:

- store it up for later until the event is just a distant memory
- jump in too quickly, when someone is still in emotional tatters at the end of an event.

Finally

How do you rate in terms of giving constructive feedback? How many of the points above can you say you honestly do when you give feedback on your team's performance?

Summary

Today you looked at some of the more personal skills you need for HRM. You looked at the importance of the role of drawing up key result areas and the contribution that standards and targets can make.

You also looked at the vital issue of giving constructive feedback.

Tomorrow you move on to the law and how it impacts on your HRM role.

Working with the law

Yesterday you looked at your personal HRM style. But however you operate you have to stick within procedures and the law. Today will give you the chance to get an overall picture of what's involved and where you have to be careful when working in any activity that is covered by laws affecting human resource management.

The bottom line is that when you are managing human resources you cannot act in a way that breaks the law. You must never put expedience before what is right or you risk damaging the staff, the organisation and yourself.

Shift it

A timber works used hydraulic lifts to get the finished materials onto the delivery trucks. The lifts were there as part of a safe system of working, but they broke down.

To get a rush order out, a supervisor instructed workers to carry out the operations manually. When they refused because there was a known risk of back injury, the supervisor said, 'there's a lot of people out there who would like your job, so think about it!'

One worker slipped a disc and sued. The health and safety inspectorate also prosecuted the firm. The supervisor was deemed to be largely responsible and the top management he was trying to please by getting the work finished dismissed him for gross misconduct.

Legal constraints

The law can be something of a moving target – especially when it comes to employment and HRM.

Any book that tells you what the law requires you to do is probably going to be out of date before it's printed. For instance:

- trade union law changed often during the 1980s – pieces of legislation were constantly changing and extending what came before
- health and safety legislation and regulations are constantly under review, both in the UK and from the EC
- court case decisions set precedents and alter the situation – recent cases include the rights of part-time employees and the right to sue for damages when a job causes unnecessary stress.

You are not expected to be an expert on all the legal niceties of work. What matters is that you know:

- what applies to you
- what the law specifies you must or must not do
- who to go to, to get detailed advice and guidance.

Show off your knowledge

Write down all the legislation that applies to your operations at work – just the titles or the areas they cover will do.

The main laws and regulations that are likely to concern you directly are those that the personnel specialist can advise on, and include:

- Sex Discrimination Acts 1975 and 1986
- Race Relations Act 1976
- Data Protection Act 1984
- Health and Safety Acts and regulations.

So, the first point to bear in mind is that it is worth seeking out the 'expert' where you work, so you can keep a dialogue going with them. If there isn't anyone, look in the phone book and make contact with your local Job Centre and Health and Safety Executive office. They will be able to provide you with detailed information and masses of free leaflets.

Remember, though, that although someone else may be the expert, many of the laws affecting HRM are the responsibility of every manager. You can't pass the buck, delegate responsibility or claim ignorance as an excuse.

There are dozens of other laws that your organisation has to handle, some of which lead to procedures that you work to. But, unless you are a personnel or wages specialist the chances are that someone else deals directly and on your behalf with issues like the:

- Disabled Persons (Employment) Acts 1944 and 1958
- Equal Pay Act 1970
- Employment Protection Act 1975
- Employment Protection (Consolidation) Act 1978

You do need to know where to go to get clarification about your own work and your own position. This underlines the importance of finding out who to ask, and sorting out with them what they handle and what you need to know about.

Why stick to the law?
The answer might seem stupidly obvious; it's because you have to. But you shouldn't stop there.

The problem is that human nature tends to operate so that anything imposed on you from outside is automatically seen as a nuisance and an interference. But the fact that something is a legal requirement doesn't mean it's stupid or that it puts you at a disadvantage – quite the reverse.

Look on the positive side and you'll see there are very sound reasons indeed for taking laws at work seriously. Look at the way two sets of issues balance out:

1 Discrimination

Anyone who discriminates against an ethnic group or someone with a disability obviously acts unfairly to them and that's against the law...

however, on the other side of the coin...

... it's good business sense not to discriminate, law or no law, because the person who makes false assumptions and discriminates loses the chance to get the widest range of skills and talents available.

2 Health and safety
Sound health and safety is obviously for the benefit of
employees…

however, on the other side of the coin…

… it's good business sense anyway, to remove or
reduce the absenteeism and sickness of skilled people
and cut out a whole range of other costly and
distressing factors.

The main areas to watch

Some of the main aspects of the law that do affect managers
are mentioned here. However, even though the following is
broadly accurate at the time of writing, you can't assume it
is directly applicable to your own situation or has not been
overtaken by further regulations. Always check! Only the
law itself gives you the correct answers and it is your
responsibility to keep yourself up-to-date.

Racial discrimination
In virtually all situations it is illegal to discriminate against individuals or groups on the grounds of race, ethnic origin or country of origin. Everyone, whatever the colour of their skin, their family history or country of origin, has the right to an equal chance when going for a job, promotion, training or other opportunity.

It is wrong to discriminate *in favour of* any one group, too. Acting to favour one group automatically discriminates against someone else, except in rare and special cases where the law says there are grounds for claiming a 'Genuine Occupational Qualification' under a specific clause in the Act. For instance, a job working in the community with people whose first language is not English could require the ability to speak Urdu. However, this sort of situation must be thought through carefully, a strong supporting case put forward and formal approval sought, so always consult the expert before taking any such action.

There are two sorts of discrimination, direct and indirect.

Direct discrimination Is often obvious, for example when someone says they want only white (or black, or Asian, or whatever) candidates for a job, or only invites people from one ethnic group to put in for a promotion.

Indirect discrimination This is generally more subtle, and is where someone devises requirements that are not essential for the job and are harder for a particular group to meet. So, saying you want an employee with blue eyes works in favour of white candidates. But it is very unlikely to have any real bearing on their ability, unless the job is to model a particular shade of eye shadow. It is quite likely to be judged as indirect discrimination. Specifying parts of a city as the only ones you will or won't recruit from is another example, if the area is populated predominantly by one particular group.

Tell your friends

There are cases where an employer with vacancies did not advertise but told the existing workforce to invite their friends to apply. Sometimes this is an acceptable way of recruiting, but where the existing workers are largely from one ethnic group, word of mouth is going to spread only amongst other people from the same group. Where this has happened it has been deemed to be indirectly discriminatory.

Equal opportunities

The same basic rules apply to gender and marital status as apply to race. Discriminating on these grounds is illegal, and there are the same direct and indirect categories.

Direct discrimination is where there are no grounds for believing that only a man or woman can do the job, but the stipulation is made anyway. Common myths exist amongst employers who believe they are exempt from the law because of:

- heavy work being involved
- situations where all or most of the current workforce is already only of one sex
- lack of existing toilet facilities for women.

None of these has any bearing on the ability of the individual to do the job – and that's what counts.

Data protection

More and more human resource data is held on computers, and anyone holding personal information in this way must register the fact. They also have to conform to eight principles on which the Data Protection Act is based:

1 Information held on individuals is obtained and processed fairly and lawfully.
2 Personal data is held only for specified and lawful purposes.
3 Any personal data held for specified purposes is not used or disclosed in any way incompatible with those purposes.
4 Personal data held is adequate, relevant and not excessive for the purposes for which it is held.
5 Personal data is accurate and kept up-to-date.
6 Personal data is not kept for longer than is necessary for the specified purposes.
7 Individuals are entitled at reasonable intervals, and without undue delay or expense, to:
• be told by the data user whether any personal data about them is being held
• have access to that data
• have it corrected or erased, where appropriate.
8 Appropriate security measures are required to protect personal data against unauthorised access, alteration, disclosure, destruction or accidental loss.

Health and safety

Everyone at work is responsible for health and safety. It isn't someone else's job – it's yours. Both the organisation (the employer) and its employees have responsibilities under the law, including the Health and Safety at Work Act 1974.

Managers, of course, get caught both ways. They're employees and they're also representatives of the organisation.

Employers are responsible
The responsibilities here are broad and cover all sorts of individuals and groups. The rule of thumb is that there is a responsibility for anyone who may be affected by what the organisation makes or does. This includes:

- all workers, whether permanent, temporary, full- or part-time, contracted or subcontracted, casual or anything else you can come up with, including people on work experience
- anyone visiting the workplace or using its equipment
- people in the neighbourhood who experience the results of the processes used, like noise, smoke, fumes and so on
- the people using the goods and services they make or supply.

There's not really anyone else left, when you think about it. To ensure that the right level of protection is in place for all these people, employers have to put in place a number of measures.

Test out your health and safety knowledge

Which of these is an employer required by law to provide and maintain?

	Yes	No
Healthy and safe materials, equipment and systems of work	❐	❐
Safe and healthy arrangements for handling, storing and transporting goods of all sorts	❐	❐
A healthy and safe environment – clean and well-lit toilets, stairs, walkways, means of access and exit, etc.	❐	❐
A written safety policy	❐	❐
Notification of any commercial or industrial undertaking to the Health and Safety Inspectorate	❐	❐
Records of injuries and occupational diseases	❐	❐
Employers' Liability Insurance	❐	❐
Opportunities for union representatives to be consulted on health and safety issues, like training	❐	❐
A system of risk assessment carried out by all managers	❐	❐

They all need a tick in the 'yes' box. When a firm is less than five people there is some flexibility in specific areas like safety policy, but generally they're all required and are all good practice.

The above list doesn't claim to be complete, either. A few more examples (that still don't complete it) are:

- some industries have their own very specific requirements
- there are specific regulations covering anyone using visual display units or computer screens
- it is a requirement to have detailed management arrangements, including risk assessment
- you may have heard of regulations covering the 'control of substances hazardous to health', commonly referred to as COSHH; such substances are found everywhere at work, so the regulations may well apply to you directly.

We suggest strongly that you get hold of a copy of relevant and specific publications, like *Essentials of Health and Safety at Work* and/or *Successful Health and Safety Management* published by the Health and Safety Executive, to make sure you know as much as you need to about the whole business of health and safety and your responsibilities. Ask your health and safety officer or your personnel people for advice and guidance. If you're stuck, ask the Health and Safety Executive. They're in the phone book and they'd rather help you get it right than have to chase you when it goes wrong.

Employees are responsible
Employees can't just sit back and leave it to the employer, though. They're responsible too. It says in the Health and Safety at Work Act that:

It shall be the duty of every employee while at work to take reasonable care for the health and safety of himself and of other persons who may be affected by his acts or omissions at work.

So, as an employee, you and the people in your team have to:

- work in a responsible, safe and healthy way
- consider the effects of your actions and omissions on groups and individuals in the same way as your employer does
- co-operate with your employer in their efforts to keep within the law; this might mean going on a special course and it certainly means not misusing or interfering with anything that is there to promote health and safety.

Summary

Today has demonstrated that there are some key areas of law that affect human resource management. Sticking to the law is not an option – it's an essential. Breaking the law means not only leaving yourself open to legal action – it's simply bad practice. You shouldn't have to depend on illegal and wrong actions to run any organisation.

Drawing the threads together

Today you are going to look at one last issue, procedures, and then look back over the week and tie all the strands together.

Procedures matter

Everything you have seen this week has been about positive moves to make your human resource role less problematic. The last new issue for you to look at doesn't always seem positive and constructive, but it is.

Discipline and grievance are issues that can feel negative, confrontational and awkward, and to an extent that's natural. After all, they are both the result of a problem. In fact they're both about grievance – one is a grievance the employer has about the individual employee and the other is a grievance the employee has about the employer.

The point to bear in mind is that formal grievance and discipline procedures are there to solve a problem or stop it escalating. In some ways, they're a form of 'heavy' constructive feedback. The purpose of any manager starting a disciplinary procedure is not to make someone's life hell, unless they model their style on Attila the Manager. The purpose is to stop the problem from continuing or happening again, by:

- letting the employee know where their performance is below standard
- explaining why that matters and the effect it has
- coming to an agreement that the unacceptable

behaviour will cease, maybe with some support through training
- spelling out the implications if it doesn't cease.

How would you feel?

How would you feel if you started disciplinary procedures against someone who had started to turn up late two or three times a week... only to find that their partner had been made redundant, so they'd had to sell the car, and the bus company had changed the timetable so they physically couldn't guarantee getting there on the dot?

You may say they should have said something, but sometimes people are shy of talking about their personal problems or don't want to be seen to be making excuses, and try their best. The answer to a case like this isn't discipline, because it won't solve the problem. It would be better to look for creative solutions, like letting them start and finish ten minutes later, or letting them take a shorter lunch break, or even reducing their working week by an hour in total, if that's the only option.

Stick to the rules

Unfortunately, some people do invoke grievance procedures or have to be disciplined, and this is where the clear and defined stages in procedures matter. It's vital to follow them to the letter, especially in discipline where a mistake could end up in an industrial tribunal. The reason is simple. Disciplinary procedures have dismissal as their last ditch and anyone who claims unfair dismissal could well be on firm ground unless you can prove that:

- they did what you say they did, and failed to make the required improvements in their behaviour
- the process of disciplining them was fair and reasonable.

In other words, you not only have to show their behaviour was unacceptable; you also have to prove you carried out the required procedures fairly and properly. There have even been court decisions where someone sacked for theft and later found guilty in court has won a case for unfair dismissal – clearly not because they were innocent, but because the procedure was not followed through. The court decided they had not been treated as they had the right to expect.

Here are two tips that might help you:

1 Put yourself in someone else's shoes and ask, 'How would I expect to be treated?' Would you expect the procedures to be adhered to, so you had all the available opportunities to make your case and sort out the problem? If the answer is 'yes', don't treat other people any differently.

2 Think about the last time you looked at the procedures they gave you when you started work. The chances are you haven't looked at the disciplinary or grievance procedures because you tucked them away at the back of the drawer months or years ago. Get them out and read them – they're standards that you are expected to follow as a human resources manager.

Round-up time

So, you have worked your way through the week. The aim has been to equip you with a variety of tools and approaches to help you manage HRM effectively.

You have looked at:

- human resource planning for today
- forecasting and drawing up a human resource plan based on changes in the future
- identifying training and development needs and drawing up a plan
- the human side of HRM, including key goal areas and giving feedback
- working within the law
- the need to stick to rules and procedures.

Put together, these areas should help you to become a modern manager able to deal with HRM and not just run away from the bits you don't like. You should be in control.

For the rest of today you will just refresh your memory of the main points and pull together your thoughts and plans.

Human resource planning for today
On Monday you looked at how a vital first step is to ask some important questions:

1　What would happen if there weren't enough people?
2　What would happen if there were too many?
3　What would happen if the number was right, but they had the wrong mix of skills?

The simple answer to all these questions is:

We'd be in trouble.

So, you need to put together a simple plan that will help you to get:

- the right number of people
- with the right skills
- in the right place
- at the right time.

This will allow you to start feeling confident and seeing where you have gaps. And when you identify the gaps you can start to do something about them. We looked at a couple of key points here.

Key points

You should:

- examine your operations regularly to make sure there are enough people in all parts of the process. Look out for overtime and other costly options.
- make sure you don't have too many people – look around with a fresh eye and try and see the situation objectively.

Now use the following box to write down any gaps or problems you identified and your plans to overcome them. You can use the plans and research you did on Monday to help you.

Gaps and problems   **Plans to overcome them**

Planning for tomorrow

But as you saw, the world changes quickly and today's plans may be in tomorrow's waste bin – at least that is unless you take the future into account first.

> ## So, successful HRM means:
>
> * anticipating human resource needs so that you aren't caught out by concentrating only on the here and now
> * putting together a human resources plan.

To do this you need first to forecast – to make a best guess – based on past experience, knowledge and extrapolation. And once you know the forecast you can plan accordingly, either drawing up initial plans or revising what you have already decided.

You looked on Tuesday at how to forecast using PESTLE analysis and then at how to draw up your plan using the following headings:

1 Our current objectives and any likely changes
2 Number of people required to deliver the objectives, broken down as appropriate into job roles, functions and tasks
3 The skills needed by those people in those roles
4 The gaps between what there is and what we need
5 Potential for retraining and upgrading skills
6 Suggested action to bridge all the gaps

Get the forecast you prepared on Tuesday and the plans that resulted in front of you. Now look through them and pull out:

- the major issues you uncovered in the forecast – what events are on the horizon?
- your main objectives
- the number of people you feel you need and the skills they need
- any gaps and how you intend to fill them.

Was there anything unexpected you came up with when you did this exercise? If so, what did you learn?

Training and development needs

On Wednesday you moved on to training and development plans for the organisation and for a particular occupation. With this big picture you can start tailoring training and development plans to the needs of individuals – your people.

A vital weapon in the armoury of any manager is *appraisal*. It is at the appraisal stage that you can really hone down the training and development plans. Performance appraisal is perhaps the most powerful way of checking on individuals' training and development needs.

The important thing with training and development is to use it wisely and efficiently. You can use the following check-list to help you judge.

A training and development activity is only worthwhile if it:

- solves a problem
- increases the level of knowledge of the employee
- raises the individual's technical competence
- adds to their range of personal skills and the extent of their self-awareness
- makes complex issues simpler and easier to understand
- allows for continuous improvement.

Why not apply these criteria to your training and development at the moment? How do you rate? What can you do to improve things, if improvements are needed?

People skills
On Thursday the spotlight turned on you and on the way you communicate with and handle people within your HRM role. Put simply, all the systems in the world are only as good as the person making them work.

The main areas you looked at were:

- clarifying key result areas
- helping people through the use of standards and objectives (targets)
- giving constructive feedback.

Pick one of the areas above and write down how effective you are at the moment and how you could make improvements.

The law
The bottom line here is that when you are managing human resources you cannot act in a way that breaks the law. You must never put expedience before what is right or you risk damaging the staff, the organisation and yourself.

So answer the following questions:

What laws affect your work?

How would you describe your knowledge of the legal position?

What laws do you need to find out more about?

Where can you go to for information?

Procedures
Finally, you saw why discipline and grievance are just as constructive and positive as all the other aspects of the role, if they're approached in the right spirit. You also looked at why procedures matter.

Try and write out the main points in your key procedures. If you have any trouble at all, get them out, study them in detail and make sure you're 100% familiar with them.

Summary

So, by working through the week and reviewing all the key points today, you should now have a clear picture of your HRM role.

The main points to bear in mind are that:

- HRM is not someone else's job – it's a partnership in which you play a crucial part
- most of the part you play in HRM comes down to thought, planning and a careful, common-sense approach

- the other part of the partnership is the expertise that personnel and other specialists can share with you
- every aspect of the HRM role is a positive and constructive one, whether it's recruitment or discipline – the aim being to identify and kill off problems at the earliest possible stage.

There's a lot in this book, so you may want to go back and look at a particular point again. Always remember the partnership and don't hesitate to talk to the specialists where you work and get their guidance, if you need to go more deeply into any HRM issues. Their aim is the same as yours – to nip problems in the bud – and they'd always rather help at the outset than help you pick up the pieces if things go wrong.

Further *Successful Business in a Week* **titles from** Hodder & Stoughton and the Institute of Management all at £5.99

0 340 59856 5	Finance for Non-Financial Managers ❐	0 340 57522 0 Successful Motivation	❐
0 340 63152 X	Introducing Management ❐	0 340 55538 6 Successful Negotiating	❐
0 340 62742 5	Introduction to Bookkeeping	0 340 64341 2 Successful Networking	❐
	and Accounting ❐	0 340 52876 1 Successful Presentation	❐
0 340 63153 8	Managing Information ❐	0 340 64761 2 Successful Problem-Solving	❐
0 340 62737 9	Succeeding at Interviews ❐	0 340 56531 4 Successful Project Management	❐
0 340 60896 X	Successful Appraisals ❐	0 340 56479 2 Successful Public Relations	❐
0 340 60893 5	Successful Assertiveness ❐	0 340 62738 7 Successful Purchasing	❐
0 340 57640 5	Successful Budgeting ❐	0 340 57523 9 Successful Selling	❐
0 340 59813 1	Successful Business Writing ❐	0 340 57889 0 Successful Stress Management	❐
0 340 59855 7	Successful Career Planning ❐	0 340 64342 0 Successful Teambuilding	❐
0 340 62032 3	Successful Computing for Business ❐	0 340 58763 6 Successful Time Management	❐
0 340 62740 9	Successful Customer Care ❐	0 340 61889 2 Successful Training	❐
0 340 65488 0	Successful CVs ❐	0 340 62103 6 Understanding BPR	❐
0 340 63154 6	Successful Decision-Making ❐	0 340 66444 4 Understanding Business on	
0 340 62741 7	Successful Direct Mail ❐	the Internet	❐
0 340 64330 7	Successful Empowerment ❐	0 340 56850 X Understanding Just in Time	❐
0 340 59812 3	Successful Interviewing ❐	0 340 61888 4 Understanding Quality Management	
0 340 60895 1	Successful Leadership ❐	Standards	❐
0 340 65503 8	Successfully Managing Change ❐	0 340 58764 4 Understanding Total Quality	
0 340 57466 6	Successful Market Research ❐	Management	❐
0 340 55539 4	Successful Marketing ❐	0 340 62102 8 Understanding VAT	❐
0 340 60894 3	Successful Meetings ❐		
0 340 61137 5	Successful Mentoring ❐		

All Hodder & Stoughton books are available from your local bookshop or can be ordered direct from the publisher. Just tick the titles you want and fill in the form below. Prices and availability subject to change without notice.

To: Hodder & Stoughton Ltd, Cash Sales Department, Bookpoint, 39 Milton Park, Abingdon, Oxon, OX14 4TD. If you have a credit card you may order by telephone – 01235 831700.

Please enclose a cheque or postal order made payable to Bookpoint Ltd to the value of the cover price and allow the following for postage and packaging:

UK & BFPO: £1.00 for the first book, 50p for the second book and 30p for each additional book ordered up to a maximum charge of £3.00.

OVERSEAS & EIRE: £2.00 for the first book, £1.00 for the second book and 50p for each additional book.

Name: ....

Address: ....

....

If you would prefer to pay by credit card, please complete:

Please debit my Visa/Mastercard/Diner's Card/American Express (delete as appropriate) card no:

☐ ☐ ☐ ☐ ☐ ☐ ☐ ☐ ☐ ☐ ☐ ☐ ☐ ☐ ☐ ☐

Signature .... Expiry Date ....